21st Century
Basic Skills
Library

I KNOW GYMNASTICS

by Annabelle Tometich

Cherry Lake Publishing • Ann Arbor, Michigan

Published in the United States of America
by Cherry Lake Publishing
Ann Arbor, Michigan
www.cherrylakepublishing.com

Consultant: Marla Conn, Read-Ability

Photo Credits: Thinkstock, cover, 1; North Wind Picture Archives, 4; Galina
Barskaya/Shutterstock Images, 6; Jeff Roberson/AP Images, 8; Laura
Stone/Shutterstock Images, 10; Aspen Photo/Shutterstock Images, 12, 14;
AP Images, 16; Kevork Djansezian/AP Images, 18; Margaret Bowles/AP
Images, 20

Library of Congress Cataloging-in-Publication Data
Tometich, Annabelle, 1980-
  I know gymnastics / Annabelle Tometich.
     pages cm. -- (I know sports)
  Includes index.
  ISBN 978-1-62431-400-1 (hardcover) -- ISBN 978-1-62431-476-6 (pbk.) --
ISBN 978-1-62431-438-4 (pdf) -- ISBN 978-1-62431-514-5 (ebook)
  1. Gymnastics--Juvenile literature. I. Title.
  GV461.3.T66 2013
  796.44--dc23
                                    2013006124

Cherry Lake Publishing would like to acknowledge
the work of The Partnership for 21st Century Skills.
Please visit www.p21.org for more information.

Printed in the United States of America
Corporate Graphics Inc.
July 2013
CLFA11

TABLE OF CONTENTS

History

Gymnastics has been around for more than 2,000 years. Cities in Greece had gyms. People ran, jumped, and stretched there.

8.200

k

H. BAR

SECT...

B

The parallel bars and the balance beam were **created** in the early 1800s. The events are still in the sport today.

Gymnastics became **popular** in the United States in the 1970s. People watched the sport on television during the **Olympics**.

Playing the Sport

Men's gymnastics has six events. They are floor exercise, pommel horse, rings, vault, parallel bars, and high bar.

Women's gymnastics has four events. They are balance beam, uneven bars, vault, and floor exercise.

Gymnasts do a set number of moves in each event. Judges award points based on how a gymnast did.

Records

Nadia Comaneci earned a perfect score at the 1976 Olympics. She was the first person to do this.

ATHENS 2004

Paul Hamm was at the 2004 Olympics. He earned the first men's **all-around title** for the United States.

American Gabrielle Douglas won the all-around title at the 2012 Olympics. She was the first African American to do this.

Find Out More

BOOK
Hofstetter, Adam B. *Olympic Gymnastics*. New York: Rosen, 2007.

WEB SITE
USA Gymnastics
www.usagym.org
This Web site has information about gymnastics competitions and gymnasts.

Glossary

all-around title (AWL-uh-round TYE-tuhl) an honor awarded to the gymnast with the best scores in all the events in a competition

created (kree-AY-ted) made something new

Olympics (uh-LIMP-icks) a competition for athletes all over the world

popular (PAHP-yuh-lur) liked by many people

22

Home and School Connection

Use this list of words from the book to help your child become a better reader. Word games and writing activities can help beginning readers reinforce literacy skills.

around	during	moves	sport
award	early	number	still
balance	earned	people	stretched
bars	events	perfect	than
based	first	personal	there
beam	gyms	points	this
became	has	ran	today
been	how	score	watched
cities	jumped	set	won
do	more	six	years

Index

About the Author

Annabelle Tometich worked as a sportswriter at the *News-Press* in Fort Myers, Florida, for six years, winning five awards from the Associated Press Sports Editors. She has also written for the U.S. Olympic Committee's Web site, TeamUSA.org. She lives in Fort Myers with her husband and son.